Now Is Not A Good Time

NOW IS NOT a good TIME

Poems by PAULA RUDNICK

Copyright © 2022
by Paula Rudnick
ISBN: 978-0-578-33153-9
Printed in the United States of America

Cover design and illustrations by Yvonne M. Estrada

for the committed activists who give me hope

CONTENTS

I. HERE AND NOW
YOU FIRST	5
SING FOR YOUR SUPPER	6
SOLITAIRE	7

II. NOW AND THEN
STING LIKE A BUTTERFLY	11
ALL THE LITTLE SOLDIERS	12
MASTER CLASS	13
FOUNDLING	15
ONLY CHILD	17
SNAKE PIT	18
WAY TOO	19
LOVE ON TOAST	20
REBEL MOM	21
GENERATION SKIPPING TRUST	23

III. NOW IS THE TIME FOR ALL GOOD MEN TO COME TO THE AID OF THEIR PARTY
WAR TORN DADDY	27
LOVE SANDWICH	28
CARD SHARK	30
RECIPE FOR GOODBYE	31
PATRICIDE	32
UNVEILING	34
VISITATION	35

IV. NOW WHAT
SALTWATER KISSES	39
MODESS... BECAUSE	40
INITIATION	41

	CONFESSION	42
	NO EXIT	43
	JANES	45
	PUSSY HAT	46
	AT THE END OF THE DAY	47
	MEN BEHAVING BADLY	48
	POV PENELOPE	49
V.	**NOW I'M GETTING IT**	
	TEA PARTY	53
	FISH TALE	54
	SINCE THE REAL ONE GOT AWAY	55
	CINEMA PARADISO	57
	SINS OF THE FATHER	58
	MOTHER-IN-LAW	59
	WITH A TWIST	61
	SHOPPING FOR A SON-IN-LAW	62
	INFIDELITY	64
	SEATING CHART	65
	GPS	66
	DOCTOR, DOCTOR	67
	BASAL CARCINOMA	68
	WARTS AND ALL	69
VI.	**NOW I'M LOSING IT**	
	SELFIE	73
	POWER OUTAGE	74
	FOGEY YOGA	75
	ELEVATOR MUSIC	76
	DOWNFALL	77
	WHAT SHOULD WE DO	78
	END GAME	79
VII.	**NOW YOU'RE KILLING ME**	
	SIDESHOW	83
	STIRRED AND SHAKEN	84

HOUSE CALLS	85
COMFORT FOOD	90
NEVERTHELESS WE RESISTED	92
AMERICAN AS APPLE PIE	94
FLOOR PLAN	95
GOD DOES STAND UP	96

VIII. I CAN SEE CLEARLY NOW

DOUBLE DOWN	99
GOLDILOCKS REPENTS	100
HEAD SHOT	101
REUNION SARAH LAWRENCE	102
LIPSTICK PARADELLE	103
THE FAMOUS POET'S WIFE	104
EMILY DICKINSON'S LINGERIE	106

AUTHOR'S NOTE

From the time I was a young girl taking Saturday morning art classes in Marblehead, Mass. to adult years making movies, hosting parties and compulsively rearranging throw pillows, my creative juices have always been fueled by a sense of dis-ease…of something being, in the immortal words of Madeline's Miss Clavel, "not right."

No generation escapes catastrophe. My grandparents lived through two world wars, my father fought in Korea, I was a seventh grader when Kennedy was shot, my children watched the Twin Towers collapse on 9/11. Cruelty, confusion and injustice are nothing new. But somehow the stakes seem higher now – the need to speak the truth and act with kindness, greater. As a small step, all proceeds from NOW IS NOT A GOOD TIME will go directly to charity.

Paula Rudnick

ACKNOWLEDGMENTS

Many thanks to the editors of the following publications who published these poems in earlier versions, some under different titles: "Initiation" – *Halfway Down the Stairs*; "House Calls" – *Moon Magazine*; "No Exit" – *Pilcrow and Dagger*; "Patricide" – *Dark House Books*; "Confession" – *Constellations*; "The Famous Poet's Wife" – *Don't Die Press*; "Side Show", "Goldilocks Repents" – *Persimmon Tree*; "Men Behaving Badly" – *Minerva Rising*; "All the Little Soldiers", "Foundling", "Snake Pit" – *The Poet*; "Love Sandwich" – *Songs of Eretz*; "Nevertheless We Resisted" – *Kosmos Quarterly*; "Comfort Food", "Fogey Yoga", "Pretty as a Picture", "GPS", "Only Child", "Cinema Paradiso", "Saltwater Kisses", "Sting Like a Butterfly", "Warts and All" – *LA Jewish Journal*

Sincere thanks to
my husband whose generosity allows me to pursue my dreams, poetic and otherwise; my daughters whose love cracks my heart; my mother for her unwavering spirit; my teachers from elementary school through Sarah Lawrence College and beyond; Deborah Stoff, my go-to beta-reader; Poets At Work writers for their feedback and encouragement; Katherine Park for her patience, enthusiasm and technical wizardry; Rose Andersen for helping me wade through years of scribbling to assemble this collection; Terry Wolverton for her guidance and many contributions to the Los Angeles literary community; Yvonne M. Estrada for cover design and illustrations, her chill snark and kind soul.

NOW IS NOT A GOOD TIME

I.

HERE AND NOW

YOU FIRST

Life's more pleasant when we're kind
emoji smile, LOL, hashtag be nice.
But you go first
because I'm having a bad day
and you parked your Jag
so close to my Toyota
I got a grease mark on my sweater
when I struggled to squeeze in
and there's a ding on the left fender
that wasn't there before
and the time it took to check it out
made free parking cost five bucks,
and shooting sprees and ice pack cracks
that make me turn to carbs
and so many other awful things
it's hard to know what part's your fault.

SING FOR YOUR SUPPER

In Homer's time the outside world
was not a finger tap away.
Beyond one's walls lay wonder,
worth defying Fates to voyage
from the place called home.
Travelers marshalled horses, chariots, boats with oars,
men to row, skins of wine to quiet fear on churning seas.
Strangers landing on a foreign shore
were welcomed with exuberance,
meat and drink laid out unsparingly,
fresh clothes offered after perfumed bath.
Not till every creature comfort was
provided did the host inquire:
Who are you? What's your quest? Tell us your story.

We want a pre-nup now
before we pour the Chardonnay,
collateral for every borrowed cloak.
Not that friends came easier for Odysseus,
caught between a rock and hard place,
lured to self-destruction by an earworm's purr,
just that tea leaves had more weight
when facts weren't free on Wikipedia.
Who knew when a grateful pilgrim
might return a kind host's favor,
share a god connection or their knowledge of the stars?
Not to mention gold, whose value stands
the test of time, just like a well-told tale.
Who are you? What's your story? We still want to know.

SOLITAIRE

Black 2 on Red 3
Black 3 on Red 4
Red Jack on Black Queen
Ace of Spades
Two of Spades
Pick a card

My mother insists on driving even though she's had two fender benders in the last three months   We beg her to take Uber but she won't   She's 94   Maybe why she's lived this long

Red 8 on Black 9
Black 9 on Red 10
Pick a card

They want to scope my husband's gut again   Maybe nothing   Maybe not   In the meantime no alcohol/sugar/spice   Sex not a problem   Ha

Red 8 on Black 9 on Red 10 on Black Jack
Ace of Hearts
Two of Hearts
Three of Hearts
Pick a card

My niece was trapped at the mall for 3 hours while police looked for an active shooter   Same thing with my daughter at another mall last month

Black 10 on Red Jack
Red 9 on Black 10

I need to stock my car with more granola bars for homeless on the freeway ramp   Beef jerky better?

Pick a card

A thousand kids in cages at the border   They must think we've stopped paying attention   Maybe we have

Red 2 on Black 3
Game over

Play again?

II.

NOW AND THEN

STING LIKE A BUTTERFLY

My mother laid it out for me:
even changed into a butterfly
I'd still have a caterpillar's face.
Geisha-fluttering in summer gardens
or blossom-shopping on a pastel breeze
I'd always be a worm at core,
essence stamped into my being
inescapable as Rorschach wings.
Leaves I crunched on pebbled sidewalks
would turn to bile in my gut
until I lost my appetite for tender things.
I'd find a mate but shouldn't
waste my time expecting romance –
reproduction fastened back-to-back
an obstacle to kisses. Still,
no reason to mourn lack of love.
Love overrated as a rose's breath,
short-lived as a butterfly.

ALL THE LITTLE SOLDIERS

My grandmother promised
all the little soldiers come back in line.
My eyes were red and popcorn puffed
face a bog of tears – jilted by The One.
Get a box of pins, she said,
and a fresh raw chicken's heart.
With every other prick to flesh
say your lover's name out loud.
Her gentle eyes went storm cloud fierce,
tender touch turned witch's clasp,
magic power whisper-passed
by unarmed women through the years.
She made me vow I wouldn't share
the secret charm of how to bring
a wayward lover back to heel
or spell could lose its sting.
I followed orders word for word
and sure enough, the boy came back…
at least until we split again.
Perhaps the one whose heart was pricked
was not the boy I mourned at all
but the grandmother who showed the way
to take grief's reins and kick sad's flanks
till all my hurt was drowned in dust.

MASTER CLASS

My mother taught me
tummies held in tight
lift bosoms,
Ginger ale and Coke
add pounds,
laughing at a lukewarm joke
builds closeness,
brighter lipstick
makes for brighter smiles.

I pull my stomach in
when trying on a bathing suit,
drink seltzer with a splash
of fresh squeezed lime,
smile at many things
that don't amuse me,
I keep a cherry lip gloss
in my purse.

***

My father taught me
wind speed under wings
lifts airplanes,
meat sliced cross the grain
makes it less tough,
hurt met with a lifted chin
chills bullies,
no one likes to hear
a woman whine.

I think about Bernoulli's Principle
when my plane
speeds down the runway,
about sinew patterns
when I cut a steak,
my jaw juts challenge
when a person taunts me,
I rarely ask
for tenderness.

***

My lover taught me
stroking certain spots
sparks interest,
too much perfume
makes it hard to breathe,
men get cranky
when a woman contradicts them,
bright red lipstick
conjures vampire fangs.

I'm skilled at ways to
stimulate excitement,
keep my fragrance subtle
with a dash of spice,
I smile enigmatically
at half-wit stories.
I never show my teeth
before I bite.

FOUNDLING

At some point every child
fantasizes herself a foundling,
left on a doorstep by a princess
to be raised by a simple shoemaker and his wife.

The princess mother
would not make her daughter
take the test she didn't study for
or send her to her room for talking back,
but she was banished from the kingdom
and forced to leave her infant in the care of pale imposters
who crushed her child with their ordinariness.

My father was not a shoemaker
but a hard-working sheet metal salesman,
my mother not an illiterate bumpkin
but a conventional suburban housewife.
For this I found it hard to forgive them.

Who was the real mother
that had left me with these dullards?
An artist surely, whose talent and courage
had brought vengeance upon her
leaving her no choice but to abandon me
on the flagstone walk of a ranch house,
disappeared without a trace.
No perfumed hankie stashed inside my swaddling,
no sapphire ring whose star could point me to her,
only a voice that whispered,
You are more than this.
Go inside and find the self you're meant to be,
The one I never would have left if I weren't certain
you could get there on your own.

ONLY CHILD

They were older than the other parents,
gray and pale, with consonants that gargled
when they said: *come in.*
They played Beethoven sonatas on their hi-fi
and taught us how to sing the Ode to Joy.
They didn't warn us not to color on the table
or be careful not to spill our milk
when elbows zigzagged outside lines.
The mother baked fresh strudel
when I played there
and the father watched us nibble it
with proud brown eyes.
The daughter's bed was canopied –
at its foot a flounced pink vanity
with lipstick samples from the Fuller Brush.
They let her feed real food
to her best doll in her old highchair
and write blue numbers on its arm
to show that it belonged to her –
like they did.

SNAKE PIT

Older sisters learn to bully
not with slaps to backs of heads,
but with averted eyes
and lukewarm compliments.

They keep their favors meager,
the better to be craved,
adding just a dash of bitters
to the sweetened punch.

Blazing pathways causes scars
a younger sister circumvents,
skipping along pre-tramped trails
twirling unimpeded.

Dogs nip dogs and cats scratch cats,
the snake that bites the mouse bears it no malice –
it's just hungry and a little rodent
activates its salivary glands.

Nature prods the older girl
to nibble at the younger's flesh,
sloughing weakened tissue
to expose the baby's spine.

How else will she grow strong enough
to survive a stranger's venom?

WAY TOO

there's too much of me

too much chill and too much sweat

too much sweat and too much blood

too much blood and too much scab

too much scab and too much wound

too much wound and too much whine

too much whine and too much tear

too much tear and too much mend

too much mend and too much mind

too much swollen heart

I overflow

LOVE ON TOAST

Keep it down, my father said
when I would laugh or cry.
The treble of my feelings hurt his ears.
He liked his love hard-boiled,
tightly packed inside its shell,
love that rinsed off trace-free from a plate.

I've always looked for love with curds,
soft-scrambled, garnished with a peach,
love that sticks when plates are cleared
and doesn't think I talk too loud
when my voice soaks through toast.
Love that urges, keep it up.

REBEL MOM

I never knew the rebel girl
my mother used to be –
letter-sweatered in a sailor hat,
eyes eager as New England spring.
She diapered edges after I was born
and sealed them with rubber pants
so juices wouldn't leak.
She kept her kisses bound as well,
sparking with my father over driving routes
or who put too much pepper in the stew.
I thought they locked their door
to keep us from their gossip
not their bliss.

I once found condoms
in her nightstand drawer,
the summer someone told me
rings along the jetty
were remains of prophylactics
not some sea snail skeleton.
Women groped for pleasure
in the dark pre-Woodstock
guided by instructions
graphed by experts
in a high shelved book.

Now and then mom teased a renegade peek –
the leopard two-piece
that she swiveled to the waves
pretending not to hear the clucks
of one-piece housewives
behind modesty panels,
the scarlet smile she impressed

on crystal rims of highball glasses
bright with sugared Bourbon.
She schooled me in the ways
a lady should behave
but I preferred my cocktails
strong like her

without the maraschino cherry.

GENERATION SKIPPING TRUST

In college I kissed married men
in day dark booths of bars
the way my mother feared I would
when I escaped her frown.

My grandma never told her
about fetuses expelled
unwanted by a husband
who liked nipples to himself.

Gran slipped this secret to me
on a trip we took to France
sipping cold Champagne at dusk
like we were best of friends.

She tittered as we dressed ourselves
for a fancy evening out
with a man we'd met at the Crillon that day
who owned a nightclub in Montmartre.

Let's keep this date between us,
Grandma said, rouging her lips.
What your mother doesn't know can't hurt
and besides what's done is done.

And she turned her back for me to zip
so she didn't see me frown
as I wondered what doors mom would crack
for my child years from now.

III.

NOW IS THE TIME FOR ALL GOOD MEN TO COME TO THE AID OF THEIR PARTY

WAR TORN DADDY

The army sent my father home
like a convict who had served his time.
He squinted back into civilian life,
uniform crushed into a duffle,
medals shadowed in a box.
He didn't show up with a limp
like in those war movies on tv,
just a tightness at the jawline
no amount of smiling could relax.

I turned my cheek away
to welcome his return.
After that he jabbed his kisses
as a way to protect lips.
My mother swore he'd fall onto his sword for me
but I did not see evidence
so we squared off,
two warriors who knew each other's weakness,
craving closeness, armed with bayonets.

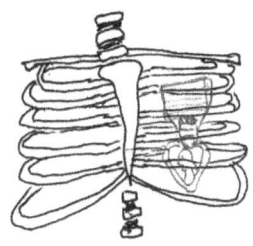

LOVE SANDWICH

When I think about my father
he's not in the Veteran's Home,
green eyes bouncing down
the rail-lined hallways
looking for his bearings.
He's at our summer house
folding sandwiches in plastic wrap
tight as Army cots,
flags of tissue wicking blood,
hoping thin sliced cold salami
will communicate his love for me
without the awkwardness of hugs.

We didn't march in close formation
on the mowed parade ground
of suburban life post-war.
Once he packed away his rifle,
he built other battlements to keep him safe
from enemy attack or friendly fire.
I tried to make him proud of me
with commendations and awards,
but when I won, I forfeited
my special spot as underdog –
the team he always rooted for
in snowy weekend football games.

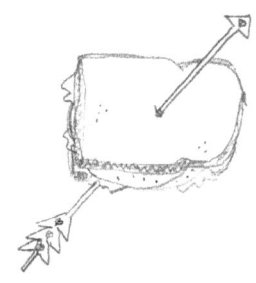

I want to climb into his lap now
so we can yell together
at the nightly news,
snap our country from the spell
of flimflam men and thieves,
show him that the values
he insisted I embody
are etched into my backbone
like the rest of what he fought for,
deep as memory of lunch meat
spread with mayonnaise and mustard
on a bruised linoleum counter.

CARD SHARK

My mother knew how to harden her heart,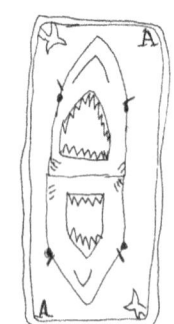
ice it the way you would any muscle
that's been overworked.
It came in handy when my father
forgot the words for chair and cheese
and who she was.

She tried to snap him out of it by yelling,
once a foolproof way to get a rise,
but now he only got confused
and told her shit, shit, shit,
which summed the situation up
more clearly than a clearer-thinking person could.

He said his hat hurt when he wore no hat,
that his shoes pinched when his feet were bare.
To maintain peace my mother made appointments
that she didn't keep with doctors who did not exist.
He'd taught her how to bluff when they were newlyweds,
poker champs for two years running
at the Fort Huachuca Officers Club.

RECIPE FOR GOODBYE

Once they swapped the twin bed
for the roll-away with rails on the side,
my father mustered for that twilight
where they say people can hear you
even if they don't respond,
it felt safe to say things I'd resisted,
finally opening his shuttered door.

I'd brushed aside his kisses
on the gangway of back home,
cut his sea legs at the knee
cold-hearted with a toddler's pout,
my love not easily captured
as a foreign enemy tank.

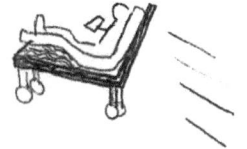

Hip to hip inside the rest home now,
we looked at glossy cookbook photos –
multi-hued terrines and stews, French pinwheel tarts.
That looks good, he said, eyes hungry,
like I was flying him to Paris on a used electric bed.
We turned the page. I held his hand.
The bones still warm.

PATRICIDE

This is how I'd kill my father:

Take him out for yogurt
at the mall near the dementia place,
order him a chocolate cone,
slide pills into the swirls.
He'd want to share, too big for one,
but I'd just say *eat what you can*
then watch him take another bite,
the way he puts one foot before the other
without knowing where he's going.

Is this my life now? he asks sadly
when we drop him in the room
with the chair he doesn't sit in
and tv he doesn't watch.
He doesn't understand
how his clothes got in the closet
or why the rest of us can leave
when they take him down to dinner.
He's mad that the attendants make him
brush his teeth and change his pants,
and he can't shave inside the dining room at lunch.
Of course you can't my mother says.
She talks to him like he's still real.

I was hoping for a blood clot
when they called to say he fell,
a bubble to his brain
to take him out,
but he was fine.
His legs weep fluid,
drenching pants and socks,

the fleece-lined scuffs he slides around in –
grizzled phantom in a terry robe.

Eat your yogurt I would tell him
if I didn't lose my nerve,
resigned to soldier on like he is
one foot past the other,
till the white flag's hoisted
and it's safe to carry off our dead.

UNVEILING

We stand next to the wall of bodies,
plug the silence between landing jets:
Gorgeous day.
He didn't suffer.
I like your hair that way.
My husband says the Kaddish.
We remember my father's casseroles,
plumbing disasters,
polyester suits.
Back at the house,
cabbage and corned beef
frozen while he was still alive.
My mother says she isn't sad. Nothing lasts forever.
My daughter hugs me in the hall.
What if you don't let people know you love them enough?
Her forehead puckers. She has his eyes.
It's always enough, I say. *And never enough.*
She blows her nose in one of his old handkerchiefs.
Don't ever leave.

VISITATION

When my father comes to visit
he's not nervous like before.
I've got a world of time, he jokes,
floating on the sofa back,
ankle crossed at knee.
He has the linen shoes on
that don't hurt his feet,
his Property of U.S. Army sweatshirt,
West Point ring.
I tell him that my sister
wears that ring around her neck.
She rubs its rim for comfort
when she's sad.
He's happy he has pleased her
with a last bequest,
that he can be of service
even in this ghostly state.
*I gave you less because you never
seemed to need my help*, he says.
Like I should take that as a compliment.

IV.

NOW WHAT

SALTWATER KISSES

Swampscott, Scituate, Cotuit –
ragged towns on rugged coast
softened by the sun.
Ocean tides and noontime whistles
measured summer's taffy days,
nighttime cricket legs rubbed love songs,
sunburns peeling under sheets.

Milton, Mashpee, Mattapan –
my grandfather's cigar butt
clamped between his yellow teeth,
gentle jellyfish in current
bubbled up from somewhere sweet
stroking out toward the horizon
in a hat crisped stiff by hot Julys.

Dennis, Sandwich, Harwichport –
Ray Charles could not stop loving me
mellow from the snack bar
on a breeze of something fried,
my name spelled out in scallop shells,
mother knitting next year's sweater
on a beach chair scribed in sand.

Plymouth, Falmouth, Yarmouthport,
pleated plaids replacing swimsuits
on the metal rounder racks at Zayre's,
August packing up her beachhead,
towels ready for the wash,
I pressed my body to their striping
not ready to rinse off the salt.

MODESS… BECAUSE

They held bouquets or champagne coupes
in slender manicured fingers,
hair chignonned or caught mid-bounce
in cloudless flowered meadows.
Their pitches never mentioned
what was being sold, an inside joke –
knowledge of the setup crucial
for the punchline to hit home.
Lashes lowered over strapless gowns,
airbrushed women broadcast secrets
over knowing smiles.

I was eight, ignorant
of grievous shames to come,
not that I was stranger to embarrassment –
my large front teeth and sweaty upper lip,
the way my face blushed cherry
when I missed a step.
I didn't realize my body
would betray me further
with its stain and stink,
my ugly essence leaking
from an unwashed place.

When I asked my mother
what the cardboard cylinders
inside her dresser drawer were for
she told me: women's toilet paper.
Why would her woman's body
need a smaller roll of tissue
than my girlish one?
Modess had the answer
but refused to share,
message tendered in a veiled code:
….Because.

INITIATION

The summer I was on the cusp
of Candyland and Kotex
the teenage daughter of a family friend
taught me how to do the Twist.

Cross-legged on her double bed
I eavesdropped as she talked to boys,
laughter simmered in her throat,
trouble in her sly jade eyes.

I watched her as she changed her clothes
from baby dolls to halter top
exhaling ghostly O's of smoke
from skinny menthol cigarettes.

We harmonized to Bobby Vee
transistor radio cranked up high,
ignoring my mom's strict advice
she shaved my furry freckled legs.

One full-mooned balmy August night
watching mating hermit crabs
in headlight glare of her MG
I slipped on sea-slick jetty rocks.

We raced for stitches in the dark,
top-down screaming, wind-whipped hair.
She teased I'd always have a scar
to remind me sex can be a bitch.

I winced a grin from shotgun seat –
I knew the score before the game:
induction into womanhood
is chaperoned by blood.

CONFESSION

It wasn't that I was a Jew for Jesus

just that I loved
the vaulted ceilings
and the organ swell
the wine and wafers on extended tongues

the incense and the gold embroidery
Caesar's language live on priestly lips
lace mantillas and the sad-faced carving
pinned onto a cross below jeweled windows

fur-trimmed stockings on December mantles
foil angels nestled in spiced spruce
list of gifts I shared with Santa
sitting on his knee at Jordan Marsh

pastel Easter bonnets, Lenten ash
pressed by thumbs to earnest foreheads
burger sacrifice to Friday fish
silver crucifixes on devoted necks

soothing notion that another being
cared enough about my future
to dry clean the smudge
of all my mortal sins

NO EXIT

flattery will get you anywhere –
to a grungy room in Paris
with a knife against your throat
as an example
locked door
no point screaming
traffic pounding down below
louder than a heart
stupid
stupid
stupid girl
thinking you're the one
who's driving
let him lick you
have you
take you
fly away
like rides to Boston
parents sniping
sister singing
melting clumps of sanded snow
crouching low along the turnpike
rolling tires chanting Om
till you're soaring
disconnected
from the buttocks
thrusting
grunting
soiling rotted mildewed mattress
months-old brie and weeks-old garlic
auburn hair across the pillow
all that's left of nerve and sinew
rest inside a navy car coat

red plaid satin lining sagging
floating high above the ceiling
of a Chevy station wagon
fever turned to frost

JANES

(Before Roe v. Wade, women formed an underground to help others end unwanted pregnancies. They all went by the name Jane.)

Plain Janes and Jane Doe's,
grizzled Janes post Fun With Dick,
quiet Janes clearing waitress throats
to let you know they were ready for your order,
housewife Janes and student Janes,
nurse Janes on their day off from the clinic,
teacher Janes who empathized
when men left tire marks after a joyride.

Janes didn't ask
What were you wearing?
Did you have too much to drink?
Don't you know
you're beautiful
is different from
I've got your back?

Some Janes answered phone calls
and some Janes drove the car,
some Janes held a clammy hand
while other Janes
scraped unformed cells
from love canals,
working in the dark.

PUSSY HAT

What is pussy? the mother asks,
America still tasteless on her tongue,
its love affair with Big Mac
something she will never comprehend.
It's a bad word, her daughter says –
good and bad, terms her mother understands,
nuance hazy as Aleppo sunsets
after bombers dropped their payload.
But what is? the mother presses,
fingers working bright pink yarn
into a hat her daughter has requested
to march in streets past uniformed men with guns.
The hat is almost finished,
two seamed squares of pink
absent decoration or a tapering crown
to hug her daughter's perfect head.
An ugly hat. She could make a prettier one
but this is what American women want
to wear on their yelling walk.
Pussy means vagina, her daughter whispers,
blushing like the mother did
when she'd explained menstruation,
caught off guard by sudden streaks of blood.
The mother's eyebrows caterpillar.
Why name a hat for something
no one's meant to see? It made no sense.
To show we're not ashamed, the daughter answers,
that they can't keep us prisoners in a cave.
Her hopeful face so beautiful,
even this ugly hat looks good on her.

AT THE END OF THE DAY

At the end of the day, he said
to signal that the conversation was over,
that his mansplanation of the world to me
had reached its final sigh,

everyone isn't created equal.
God made Eve from Adam's rib bone,
something Adam could live without
at the end of the day.

Long story short? he yawned,
somebody writes the test and somebody takes the test
and at the end of the day
the person with the red pencil decides who gets the A.

People who think outside the box
get left outside the box,
he mumbled through a bite of pie.
Sorry to burst your bubble.

Know the Golden Rule?
He who has the gold
is the one that makes the rules,
all due respect.

He shrugged. *It is what it is.*
I'm talking apples
you're talking applesauce.
By the way – excellent pie.

MEN BEHAVING BADLY

In Manhattan there's a walking tour
of New York's most obnoxious men,
buildings where the power guys
and their young suited wannabes
preyed on women with a cute behind,
banging, boinking, rogering them,
smashing up against their blazers
to cop a feel of the breasts inside,
scronching, pummeling, groping
despite threat of hashtag me-too swipes,
grabbing, poking, thumping
female underlings who craved a mentor
or who needed work to feed the kids.
At 30 Rock – Bill Cosby and Matt Lauer.
Fox News – O'Reilly, Roger Ailes.
CBS – Les Moonves, Charlie Rose.
Too many in one block to name them all.
Tour of the restaurant lechers
offered Tuesdays in the autumn.
Sold out through October.

POV PENELOPE

Penelope was good at waiting.
It was difficult at first –
chillier in the morning
without Odysseus's breath
warming flattened hides,
his rowdy laughter plumping plaster,
hard muscle against pliant flesh.

But she adjusted, for Telemachus,
a boy without a father prey for scoundrels
as a queen without a king.
She had a house to run, her loom, her thoughts
which as the years slid by
proved better company
than striving suitors bent on her undoing.

She learned to value wits over her womanhood –
marriage to a soldier confirmation that
a wounded beast is likelier to strike.
She wove and rewove husband's shroud,
pulling stitches when she neared the end,
less because his death too grim to contemplate
than flow of warp and weft itself a joy –
for him of course a wardrobe for the afterlife,
but also cloak for her, a thing apart.

No man chooses to be No-man,
how Odysseus dodged the Cyclops' jaw,
but left to her devices with enough time,
a woman can unveil choices, too.

V.

NOW I'M GETTING IT

TEA PARTY

The little china tea set
with the delicate pink flowers
was given to me by an aunt and uncle
who were childless.
The blossoms were hand painted
and the porcelain was so thin
you could almost see
imaginary tea inside.

I sipped some from a tiny cup,
pinkie curled into the air,
confiding to the girl next door
details of my pretend days –
chores that left me sad and tired
with children who refused to sleep
and cried when I went out at night.
I couldn't wait till they grew up
so I could have my life again.

My playmate nodded sociably,
took another Goldfish cracker
from a paper plate,
said her kids were even worse,
especially since their father left
and started dating the babysitter.

FISH TALE

a stone's throw
from a slippery place
at unfamiliar water's edge
I cast my opalescent lure
at your quick darting shadow

near sinker's depth
you took the bait
our reeling dance began
breathless twisted tango
left you flopping at my feet

you smacked your tail
the gravel jumped
but you were at line's end
when I freed the hook
and tossed you back

not as large as you'd appeared
swimming at a distance

SINCE THE REAL ONE GOT AWAY

She misses her real husband,
the one who died.
He reneged on the forever part
and for punishment
she let another man replace him
in the hollow of her bed.

The new husband is smarter in a book-like way,
not the way she likes her smarts.
Anyone can read
but radar is a precious gift
like rhythm and an ear for tune
in the static of the universe.

Already she's begun to question
everything she learned from him,
like not to dread the dawn
and letting go with joy
the same as flying.
Foolish to have swallowed smoke.

He loved her LA eyes and New York mouth,
the way she cha-cha'd into crashing waves.
He watched her from the lifeguard tower,
steady facing riptide surf.
You said you'd save me
but I'm drowning, she cries out.

She pounds the place his chest was,
drags her nails through his empty bulk.
Her head slams thick against the ocean floor,
blood rings sand through swirling caves.
You told me you could swim, he shrugs,
and curls into the blue-lit night.

She drifts through darkened rooms
inspecting photos for a glimpse of ghost.
What's past is past, the smarter husband says. *Move on.*
Her real husband's bones are naked now
inside the box she packed him up in
sealed with a kiss and clump of earth,

herself still swaying to the pressure of his hand
at the soft indentation of her waist.

CINEMA PARADISO

My husband goes to movies
on the inside of his forehead
where he's a spy in fancy suits.
Gorgeous girls admire his abs
and bat their interest at him
behind too-long bangs.
They don't remind him that
the buttered jumbo popcorn turns to plaque
or that he shouldn't drive the get-away
so fast around the curves.
They're in it for the moment's heat,
not true-blue long-term story line.

I'd like to buy a ticket for myself
and watch him chase the villain,
foil the thief, save the universe
from evil with a rakish grin.
I'd even sit through love scenes,
buxom women scraping breasts
across his freckled belly
which looks flatter in the dark.
I'd try not to be jealous
of how hungrily he kisses them
or how he looks into their eyes
and lets them know they're beautiful.

SINS OF THE FATHER

My husband's father was a drinker.
His mother was a drinker's wife.
Hard to trust that ice of love
will hold old trauma's weight
with shards under a caterer's napkin
waiting to draw blood.

This is what my father did to me
in Boston, Poland, old Judea,
in God's garden before primal serpent
raised its flattened head.
This is how the prologued past
returns full circle with a golden ring,

why I hear: you're ugly
when my husband tells me I look tired,
why he hears: you're lost
when I tell him where to park.
It's vodka's memory that makes him turn on me in anger,
my mother's hand on frizzy bangs that makes me flinch.

MOTHER-IN-LAW

My mother-in-law asked our nanny
if she could borrow her panties.
She was sitting at the breakfast table
when she spied them drying on the rack.
They looked so fresh and clean.
She hadn't put enough inside her suitcase
when she packed it in Palm Beach.

She liked this girl,
who spoke good English,
not like the last one
with the gold tooth and the attitude.
My mother-in-law could buy her own of course,
if her stomach weren't so full of gas
it hurt to try things on.

She told the nanny of her constipation
as she watched her rinse the dishes,
confidentially, like they'd been chums for years.
She used to have such lovely things –
fur-lined coats and diamond pendants,
everything stolen while she was at the club
winning first prize in the cha-cha contest.

Her husband was a handsome man,
a good provider, but he drank too much
which made him say mean things.
She had a closet full of clothes then,
nothing with elastic waists.
Now she had to stay close to the bathroom
on account of the suppositories.

Enjoy life while you can,
she told the nanny
as the girl wiped down the kitchen sink,
and got up from the breakfast table
panties clutched against her ample bosom,
cotton jersey trophy
from her latest competition.

WITH A TWIST

We were a vodka shot from sober
when she told me that she liked
her oldest son the best,
the difficult one – tall drink of snark
with father's fire that mesmerized
back when she craved flames.
Her younger boy more la-dee-da,
his cheerful bulk immune to wind
that sculpted brother's granite glare –
a pinioned climb, but oh the view
eye to eye with her sublime creation.

It's hard for me to really say
which daughter jangles me the most.
The older one knows spongy spots –
she jabs opinions with a fencer's thrust.
Her softer sister calls for comfort
and I give advice –
we know the ways to wound each other
with a dial tone.

I'd stop a truck for either girl,
but firstborns have the starter's edge –
first tug, first pulse, first oxytocin flood,
basting stitch for all ensuing seams,
the way we still can taste our first shy kiss
long after we've let go of longing
or the tender recollection
of a young boy's tongue.

SHOPPING FOR A SON-IN-LAW

Thumping melons in organic produce
or shuffling shoeless in the line at TSA,
I scan for men to be my daughter's husband.
I'm not looking for Adonis,
the kind who needs a mirror's confirmation.
Not somebody Olympic-fit,
my baby's skin too fair for outdoor sports.
Someone with a ready smile.
Her wit can bite, not that she's dark
just that her heart's too kind
to ignore the world's injustice.

She says she's done with dating apps,
pointless virtual encounters
that climax in a coffee date
where checks are split.
Easier to leave one's fate to chance
than waste a weekend swiping right
through seas of Mr. Wrongs.
She'd be annoyed if she found out
I trawl for suitors as I drop zucchini in a plastic bag
or extricate 4 ounces of conditioner
from my rolling carry-on.

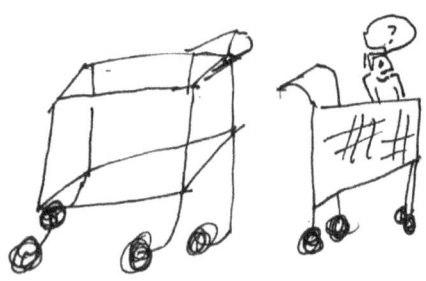

Technology has fooled a generation into thinking
they can cut through slog of courtship straight to love
but some things don't outgrow old-fashioned ways,
and while I don't presume to know what's best for her,
the guy in the plaid shirt who's asked the butcher
how to cook a piece of halibut is cute
and doesn't have a wedding ring.
I think I'll tell him it's great baked
with parsley butter in a Pyrex dish
the way I taught my daughter who's a virtuoso in the kitchen
and just happens to be single.

INFIDELITY

The Van Cleef chain link grips its pearl
in the boney canyon between saline breasts
of my girlfriend's husband's mistress.
He found her on the internet
on a site that matches lollipops
with sugar daddies looking for a suck.

She's got his Amex now
and a bag from Saint Laurent,
gifts an aging lover gives
to prove he's more appealing
than a younger, poorer guy.

My friend is interviewing surgeons
to re-tuck her tummy, lift her lids,
prepare herself for dates on Match-dot-com,
as if a blast of Botox could erase the pain
that etches on a woman's face
when her husband's texts unmask him.

SEATING CHART

I've cracked the seating for the dinner party:
the artist beside the curator
PI attorney next to divorcee
child star next to star-fucker
poet who drinks next to cellist who smokes
guy who hates Mexicans next to guy who hates Muslims
diabetic next to woman with celiac
vegan from book club beside nun who left the church
my husband as far away from the exotic dancer
as two table leaves permit

GPS

My husband takes instruction
from the GPS girl, not from me.
He puts her on before his seatbelt
to make sure he finds his way
between our driveway and the street.

He doesn't think she's bossy
when she tells him
to take Palm instead of Elm,
or U-turn back to where he started
in the middle of the road.
She doesn't get upset when he is late
or become cranky when he's lost,
just continues speaking sweetly
so he senses her support.

If she says left and I say right,
he tells me to be quiet.
She doesn't know about
construction by the park
that will coat his just-washed
Tesla S with dust
or that Doheny is one way
till Monday on account of
the gay pride parade.

In my next car, I want a manly GPS
who talks to me in Gauloises-sexy French.
It doesn't matter I don't speak the language –
I'm not really looking for directions.

DOCTOR, DOCTOR

Grizzled MD's flirt with me.
It's all innocently professional –
my husband their patient, too,
but people seek their expertise
less frequently these days,
younger patients wanting younger docs,
wives too busy with their book groups
and their golf to steal a quick lunch.

Gowned in limp blue cotton,
my damp thighs wrinkling paper,
I watch them scribble in their folders
my insomnia, weight gain, alcohol consumption,
coyly asking whether I prefer young Burgundy
to aged Bordeaux and where I'm traveling next
and who is more to blame for current national crises,
the GOP or Democrats.

They're no more turned on by my dimpled buttocks
than I am by their nose hair,
but we're alone and I am close to naked
and the finish line of adoration looms
despite their monogrammed lab coats
and my lace matching lingerie.
My med school boyfriend dumped me in my twenties.
I've been looking for a second opinion ever since.

BASAL CARCINOMA

it was just a little flap of skin not a sixteenth of an inch
nothing that a person couldn't live without

flesh removed from nose with scoop
like toasted almond fudge from frozen glass display

my fingers sticky as I made your change
creamy kisses in the parking lot after my shift

the candle dipping summer that we met
your t-shirt spiced with tallowed Bayberry

your suntanned profile undented like in photos
fading slowly on our bedroom shelf

snapped years before I searched for sores between your
    whiskers
every time you pulled me into an embrace

WARTS AND ALL

funny how the things that rankled
are the things I miss

pj's jumbled in the closet
toothpaste mountained in the sink

feather tickle that raised goosebumps
quill that pokes my heart

plastic album pages
throb with heat

you and me and mahi-mahi
Kona line-caught on a sail,

kimono costumed Halloween –
two swordless smiling Samurai

I want your slouching back
to stand up straight another time

another chance to laugh
when balled up paper misses can

habits suffered with a sigh
prickle eyelids with a smile

light blue sweater with the hole
how you called a drawer a draw

images like loam
each time I swallow

I want you back – the scars, the moles
so I'll know it's your eyes draping at the edges

your skin brined in summer waves
your lips wet with coffee kisses

your freckled constellation across dimpled cheeks
your cowlick, no one's hair can grow the same

VI.

NOW I'M LOSING IT

SELFIE

You know that feeling when you're running late and there's no hot water and you're on hold forever because everyone who doesn't want to pay a plumber time-and-a-half waits till Monday morning and when you finally make it to your car there's a ticket on the window?
I have that feeling.

The feeling I got reading Anne Frank's diary the first time thinking how hideous it would be for strangers to know when I got my period, and how sad it would be locked in an attic with my parents, all our neighbors wanting us dead.

I have the feeling there's just a few more feet at the amusement park before our roller coaster car careens. The feeling the little Dutch boy had knowing his finger in the dyke was the only thing between dry ground and drowning. The feeling ancient shepherds must have had when hail rained – that this time really was the end of times.

Maybe AA has it right. Serenity. Acceptance. One terrifying, unbearable day at a time. Screw up after screw up after screw up when the truth is clear and we've been warned: this is not the selfie God was going for.

POWER OUTAGE

I'm jammed between control-delete and caps-lock,
thwarted shifting files when I try to cut and paste.
I lose highlighted text like matching socks inside a dryer,
underline the phrases I've requested be bold-faced.
I don't know how to Share or Friend or Instagram,
forget when I'm supposed to mouse-click right or left,
I can't attach a pdf or jpg, dither whether upgrades
should be cancelled or installed.
I was once considered quite the Renaissance woman –
I could play piano, mend a hem, decorate a birthday cake
   with buttercream florettes.
I knew the proper order of the forks on formal tables,
could prune a rose bush, roast a turkey, plunge a toilet,
   lift a stain…
but staring at a glowing screen I'm terrified
one mis-hit key will undo hours of work
without a high-priced still-in-high-school expert
coaching me with steady patient prompts.
It makes me pine for thoughts of ink on paper
that will not crash before Command-shift-S
can firewall my evanescent brilliance
in the virtual safe harbor of a cloud.

FOGEY YOGA

We roll onto our sides slowly
my hip replacement
his fused spine
ankle reconstructed after sidewalk tumble
shoulder frozen in a round of golf
slipped discs trying to relocate pre-slipped slots
we whimper into downward dog
grunt through sun salute
shoulder stand a curtain of loose skin
headstand balanced between folding chairs
broken heroes posed on swollen knees
wounded warriors one and two
rounded triangles
bowing boats
final savasana
the hardest pose of all they say
demanding full cessation
of intent and doing
almost there

ELEVATOR MUSIC

We put the elevator in for later,
when pills queued on nightstands
and rubber soles squeaked through halls.
It was an item on the master plan,
like the generator to keep things
frozen when the big one hit.
It came in handy packing for vacations,
easier than dragging luggage down the stairs,
a good place to store the vacuum.
My husband didn't slink down to the guest room
to avoid my elbow when he snored then.
Bathroom mirrors smiled when I walked by.
The wine I drank at dinner didn't pool
in plums under my eyes next morning.
I remembered words to all the Beatles songs.
Before my father lost his mind
and my sister lost her breast
and our broker lost the savings
we had put away for later
when we thought life's painful steps
could be avoided in an elevator.

DOWNFALL

It's usually
a missed step
a cracked hip
a cold that settles
as pneumonia
in a hollow chest
but for my mother
it was a phone call
from a grandson
the accident his fault
the other driver pregnant
and the baby died
but the lady wouldn't sue him
if he sent her cash
and please don't tell his mother
so she mailed money
like the voice beseeched
because love makes prudent people
do imprudent things when they are 94
and live policemen aren't around when thieves
snatch purses that aren't tightly clenched
and strangers know from Instagram accounts
whose daughter's finished chemo
and whose grandson calls them GlamMa.

WHAT SHOULD WE DO

What should we do
with the body
when the dial tone goes flat
no outgoing calls
no incoming
eyes blank as an abandoned building
skin dry as weeks-old toast

What should we do
with the skeleton
when paddles lift
to claim the flatware
and tea sets
scored at foreign flea markets
brim with dregs

Where shall we store
the carapace
when thoughts
are siphoned clean
and gulls no longer bicker
over remnants
bleached of tint and tang

What should we do
with a shell that's empty
when fingers
on familiar curves
no longer raise a smile
and hands
that once helped plastic trowels
build a sandy citadel
no longer know what's sky
and what is shore

END GAME

There was no light
No tunnel
Just stars
Between my head
And ceiling
When the concrete hit
No more

My eyes were open
I did not black out
At least not
That I noticed
No awareness
Being part of it
So possibly

I wasn't frightened
Just confused
What was rain and
What was blood
Puddled
Naked
On a foreign floor

So this is how it ends
I thought
No glow
No highlight reel
Just day spa calm
Like when you snap the final piece
Into a jigsaw

And it's done

VII.

NOW YOU'RE KILLING ME

SIDESHOW

We're addicted to the sideshow –
the lady sporting whiskers,
donkey with two heads,
cotton candy frosting hair
of carny's tattooed arm.
We're hooked on big striped big top,
the popcorn and the stink,
riding crop and oil slick
of barker's red-tailed spiel.
We love to peek at freaky things
behind the velvet drape,
to hold our breath in choked suspense
as netless bodies fly.
We want to hear the lions roar,
see cars spit out more clowns,
exhale ah's of hot dog damp
when wrists are caught, or not.
We crave our penny's worth of pound,
our barrel full of Coke,
the cannonball, calliope,
cold tang of something sour.

STIRRED AND SHAKEN

Ragged cardboard
on the freeway ramp.
Homeless. Hungry. Help me.
I study dashboard dials to avoid
magic marker accusations,
ratchet radio volume high
to silence red light stare.

I lived in Montecito once
before the fires and the floods.
The Starbucks line was shorter there,
clients white as macchiato foam
floating over bitter brew.
I felt homeless, helpless, hungry
for fare I could digest.

The mind's eye tries to blind itself
but it cannot escape pictures
captured when the flash pops hot,
subject and photographer
trapped by same device,
immortalized in chemicals,
arrested at a green light's turn.

HOUSE CALLS

i.   BATTLEGROUND

The picket fence was peeling
and the drought had won its argument
with once green grass.
I placed a please-vote notice in the doorjamb,
kissing cousin to the flyer
from the Desert Vineyard Fellowship,
competing suitors for the hearts
and minds of absent souls,
crunched my way back to the sidewalk
as an SUV pulled onto concrete,
evicting a plump woman
and two dark-haired girls.

The smaller girl had baby teeth,
the older child, breast buds.
I asked the woman if
she got her sample ballot.
She sensed the question was a trick,
said her husband was a citizen and he did
hoping this would disappear me,
but I stood my ground with gritted clipboard,
aimed my stump speech at the almost-teen
heir to this star-speckled banner,
faded since my father's parents
fled pogroms to carve a brighter future
out of deli meat and sweat.

Your father can preserve this country
with his vote, I prophesied,
powerful as any millionaire's
if we all stand together for what's right.

The baby sister hopscotched up the driveway,
the mother popped the trunk.
Half bemused, half bludgeoned,
the teen agreed to be my messenger,
turned attention to the groceries
as I logged household data in my app –
Voter Disposition: Undecided.

ii. DOOR TO DOOR

We squared off in our wife beaters,
mine pleated over love handles,
his tight across a growing paunch.
He held the hose defiantly,
spitting pastel rainbows
at his patch of American dream.

His house wasn't on my walk list,
but I longed for human contact
after so many folded flyers
under so many no-one home doors.
I told him I was volunteering
for someone who wanted to protect
health care and the environment.
He told me he was a Republican
who believed in the 2nd amendment,
shifted his stream to the azaleas
barely missing my toes.

I said my candidate was a gun owner
as was her father – a cop.
He glowered ice, removed his gloves.
If he decided he wanted to strangle me,
would anyone hear me scream?
His chest was broad and hairless, vitiligo flecked,
face worn and sunbaked under flop of steel hair.

In a starched white shirt in a Westside bar,
he was the kind of guy I would flirt with.
If I were single. If he were.
If we happened to be seated next to each other
drinking Pinot Noir.

He shut the spigot, stared at my chest.
I clutched the dog tags around my neck,
said my father was an Army officer
who'd won a Bronze Star in Korea.
He said he was a Viet Nam veteran
who never saw combat, just purified water.
Still service to the country, I countered.
Like me here today.

He studied his flip flops,
mumbled he was a conservative.
I handed him a flyer. His grip was firm.
*And what is it you think we should
be trying to conserve?* I asked,
before heading down the walk.
At a Westside bar drinking Pinot Noir,
I probably would have gone home with him.

iii. KNOCK, KNOCK

Knocking doors on dusty road,
final block in target town
to flip a red state blue,
I called into the morning dark.

A slender figure stirred behind
a pockmarked screen,
more barrier to shooting spree
than bug-proof mesh,

aimed an oblong clicker
at a flickering wall –
marching bands fell silent
as he ambled toward the light.

His latte skin was tatted
with entwining navy vines,
push pin through his tongue
yawn-sparkled silver.

Yes, he said he'd registered,
and *yes*, he'd vote my way,
and *yes*, he knew to mail it,
but he took my blank form anyway

because there was no charge for it
and the halftime show was dull
and I was older than his grandma
standing out there in the heat.

I moved on to my next address
and he moved back to bed,
one more stucco cellblock
till I was home with the one percent.

It was high noon in a moonscape,
last shrunk spider crumpled
by last sorry-I-missed-you note
in last sad dirt-caked web,

I could almost hear Leonard Cohen streaming
through my Tesla Dolby dash,
when I spied a tattooed specter
waiting for me at the curb.

No dented grate between us now,
I smiled with tightened jaw
as he fished a low-slung pocket
and produced a filled-out form.

Thanks, I said, my breath returned.
He nodded his reply.
I was halfway to the freeway ramp
before the tears arrived.

COMFORT FOOD

Under a bower of old pittosporum
at a once-grand Montecito estate,
thirty women under forty
gathered to discuss the state of the world.
As usual, it was grim.
Pain and suffering across the hemispheres.
Reproductive rights once again under siege.

Despite creature comforts,
fancy educations,
successful climbs up success's ladder,
they felt powerless.
The conversation turned to brisket.
Each was convinced she
had the world's best recipe.

The hostess, a former ballerina,
said she smothered her meat completely
with thin sliced onions and carrots
till not a glimpse of flesh remained.
Her toned arms flexed gracefully
under gauzy sleeves as she spoke
thanks to good genetics and a daily Pilates routine.

The tv executive,
who had once driven her Mercedes
through a closed garage door when the clicker
   malfunctioned,
swore by her French granny's technique
of adding wine to beef and vegetables
in an old iron pot, or lacking that,
a new Le Creuset.

The CEO of a tech start-up
said she had no time to cook,
but chili sauce and Lipton's onion soup
worked miracles and it was crazy
to spend money on a fancy pot
when you could get the same result
in a cheap enamel roasting pan from Amazon.

The yoga instructor claimed
that extra-firm tofu was as good as veal
when baked with barbeque sauce
or mango chutney.
She had served it to carnivores
on many occasions and everyone
thought it was meat.

They all agreed the secret to a brilliant brisket
was to cook it low and slow
with liquid in a covered pan,
and they would reconvene the following year
for a taste-off to see whose was the best.
Each would also bring her version
of the world's best chocolate mousse.

NEVERTHELESS WE RESISTED

It isn't like they didn't try to tell us
with charts and graphs
and documentary footage
of the ice cap melting
and whales rotting homeless
on receding sand.
We had more than an inkling
of the story arc,
but we were hooked
on one-click shopping
and we didn't want to share
our fresh tomatoes with the slugs.
Besides, what point the sacrifice
of one-use plastic bottles and our Jumbo-trons
with China burning coal to keep its billions calm
and Brazilians scything down the Amazon forest?
We figured scientists would find new ways
to cool the planet off and suck
destructive gases from the air
before more CEO's lost beachfront homes,
so we trusted those who told us
everything was fine and we should go
about our business like we always had
for hadn't we taught cars to drive
and Roombas to remove the crumbs from floors?
Had we not shot men into space
and could we not ping vaycay photos
from our mobile phones?
Impossible to make us ponder
life with less as more,
erasing what we'd earned
through brain power and might,
our kissing cousin kinship with Divine.

Who could dare deny our claim
to masters of the universe –
our progress so evolved
in such short time?

The Universal Master sighed
and dialed up the heat.

AMERICAN AS APPLE PIE

America is running out of apple pie.
We've chopped down all the fruit trees
and rolled our dough down into flakes.
Our crust is sagging and our cinnamon has soured.
Four and twenty blackbirds have pecked their way into
　another anthem.

Our pie might last if we just cut it into squarer slices,
but Kindergarten so long gone, who can remember what
　we learned there?
Eensy weensy spiders too worn out to launch a climb,
easier to crawl along the bottom and wait for something
　to come trickling down.
Like Keynes expounded, better to be roughly right than
　rightly wrong.

Betsy Ross's handwork threadbare,
we lift our prayers to heaven with raised fists,
kiss the flag and whisper sad sweet nothings to its stripes.
God's on our side, and besides we've got more ammo.
Liberte! Egalite! Brother, get your ass out of my driveway.

Problems streaming nightly for our mass consumption,
we eat the things we are
and in tremendous quantity.
Axe that felled the cherry moved to thicker tree trunks
now it's clear no one is punished for a lie.

FLOOR PLAN

Don't call it the master bedroom, my daughter frowns.
It conjures the plantation. Say primary.
She's shopping for a house
and we're discussing floor plans.
Whoa, ok, I say, revising:
the primary bedroom has skimpy closets
and the primary bathroom gets no natural light.
I hide my eye roll with a blink.

But when the buyer of my mother's house,
on the market after 50 years,
insists the couch I promised to a friend
be thrown into the deal, I think, great –
now I'm an Indian giver. And I freeze.
What Indian ever reneged on a gift to me
and when did this misguided myth
dart into my lizard brain?

I'm proud of my transaction skills,
honed at Harvard Business School,
but when negotiating's billed as
Jewing someone down, my bones go cold
and I'm reminded of my place.
If there's a master bedroom there must be a master
and someone lesser bedded elsewhere –
servant, woman, slave? Someone unprimary.

GOD DOES STAND UP

God is headlining at the Comedy Club.
He flop-sweats through a thousand jokes before hitting
    his stride.
Ice cubes chill Tequila as people cough into their napkins,
French fries tickle ear lobes with their salty tongues.

Elvis has left the building in a too-tight white fringed
    jumpsuit.
He got too big for britches and his groupies lost the love.
We're all a bunch of hound dogs
thinking clapping will save Tinkerbell,

but tired motor of belief's the thing
that fuels the little engine's climb.
Cream sinks to the bottom when the bubbles pop,
God no shticky tummler bent on ass-kissing the crowd.

If Debby Downer doesn't like His act,
she won't get money back.
No one's here for funny,
we want the homemade apple strudel,

Gornisht helfn anybody hoping for a bite.
Maraschino cherries touch up lipstick at the drum roll.
God concludes his final set
to thunderous applause.

VIII.

I CAN SEE CLEARLY NOW

DOUBLE DOWN

Double negatives rebut themselves.
I'm not not going,
means I'll probably be there.
I don't not love him,
means I kind of do.
Saying things with opposites
flips them inside out,
tucking feelings under seams
to slide against the skin.
So when we jump off mountain tops
with nothing but clasped hands
and folded promises
understand I understand
it's not not dangerous.

GOLDILOCKS REPENTS

I used to swoon for older bears
in striped rep ties and wingtips,
but I've become allergic
to stuffed shirts and vested suits.
My skin breaks out in raised red welts
when bigshots flash their greenbacks,
metallic scent of silver
turns my porridge inside out.

I can taste the sweat of weavers
on my thousand thread count bedsheets.
Cozy chairs and comfy beds
no longer ease my ache.
The only Southern Comfort
that I crave these days is sunshine,
not too hot and not too bright,
tenderized in mist.

Emptiness does not get full
flirting with abundance.
Doing nothing well not what
the Buddha meant by clear.
I sit in lotus pose and trust
enlightenment to fuel me.
Spurn desire. Let the minnows
feast on others' crumbs.

HEAD SHOT

Turn your head a little to the right.
Chin down.
Good.
Left ear to left shoulder?
Your nose was blocking the light.
Chin up.
Touch more.
Yes.
Let me add some fill.
Minimize those circles.
Chin down a bit more.
Look left.
Just with your eyes.
Good.
Now lift your neck.
Like a giraffe reaching for a leaf.
Head straight.
Eyes left.
Little smile?
Good.
Less teeth. Like Mona Lisa.
Yes!
Now with everything just like it is, raise your lower lids
    up to your pupils.
Whoa – not so much. Looks like you're about to seize.
A little laugh. That's good.

                Ok, flirt with me.
                Like Julia Roberts in Pretty Woman.
                Less teeth.
                Yes.
                Hold it.
                Perfect.
                That looks so natural.

REUNION SARAH LAWRENCE

Fat hydrangeas, impossibly blue,
soothe stone-faced houses,
jaws of stars and stripes
glower over welcome mats.
Graying road, path from here to there,
cracked lifeline ready to tell fortunes.

I stroll beneath the plump wisteria,
bare-headed and un-gowned.
Birds sing oldies over frisbee'd grass.
A cry of recognition as two one-time friends embrace.
If I bumped into my sad-eyed freshman self
would I even wave?

LIPSTICK PARADELLE

Who am I without the lipstick and the answers
Who am I without the lipstick and the answers
Crouched again at starting gate
Crouched again at starting gate
Without answers crouched at starting gate
The lipstick who I am again

Muscles carved in younger days
Muscles carved in younger days
When I was proud of nakedness
When I was proud of nakedness
When I was proud of muscle days
Carved in younger nakedness

I elbowed past the obstacles
I elbowed past the obstacles
Faster than the sound of light
Faster than the sound of light
Elbowed past the sound of light
Faster than the obstacles

Who am I without my obstacles
Muscles crouched with elbowed light
Carved again from younger days
Lipstick at the starting gate
Faster than the sound of proud
Answers in my nakedness

THE FAMOUS POET'S WIFE

The famous poet's wife

studies the French-cut green beans
criss-cross stacked like pick-up-sticks
at the upper right-hand corner
of her gold-rimmed Limoges plate.

Her husband is expounding now
on truth and fate and accident
with tongue that once teased labia
in eager wheeling somersaults,

his kisses damp and muscular,
herself a newborn sonnet
lapping up his couplets
with the full creative ardor of her heart.

Bodies at the table lean in unison,
tilting toward the famous poet's baritone,
transfixed by every propelled percussed consonant,
each vowel taffy-pulled to stir a moan,

"can't" pronounced as "cahnt"
like he'd read History at Oxford,
son of British royal clan
not Julius "Ziggy" Friedlander.

The famous poet lifts his index finger,
arthritic digit maestro's poised baton,
orchestra of guests awaits his downbeat
breath on hold until they get the cue.

The famous poet's wife

chews on a bite of lamb chop.
Diners sigh applause at elegy's end,
homage to the poet's long-dead mother,
scold recast as Mary Magdalene.

"Poetry's an oral art,"
the famous poet lectures,
"intended for the ear, not for the eye"
his stump speech almost over,

vibrato rolling down the gleamed mahogany,
candle flames diagonal in the air,
wind from source so deep within his psyche,
buttons on his grease-stained silk shirt strain.

The famous poet's wife

pokes at a bean with silver fork tines,
drags it past the creamy mashed potatoes
trying not to jostle other beans,
game she plays on nights like this

to set her face with focus
that might appear as rapture to a fan
bedazzled by the famous poet's brilliance
and his metered serenades to selfless love.

EMILY DICKINSON'S LINGERIE

I'm pawing through Emily Dickinson's underwear
  looking for a metaphor.
Despite her veiled hints, I find no leather thongs there.

Her slips smell of lavender. They snag on my cuticles.
I can hear her lips moving through perfumed silk.

Emily and I both products of New England winter.
Our slips smell of moth balls and wet wool.

Some psyches don't look good in a bikini,
but googly eyes can soften sorrow's glare.

Sad that observation's gift
can doom a girl to solitary confinement.

Know what I mean? always a yes
when talking to oneself.

At least a narrow circle helps the mind to focus.
The deeper down we dive, the higher we can soar.

Emily mumbled curses as she poured hot tea in china.
Fan girl gulped it up, sweetened it with Splenda.

I've learned to cherish bitterness of simple.
Blistered flesh the loveliest to touch.

The more I read the more I want to tear my clothes off.
Verses help me locate veritas.

May white feathers
brush away my trembling.

Hope a thing of paper
swept with ink.

www.ingramcontent.com/pod-product-compliance
Lightning Source LLC
Chambersburg PA
CBHW032055150426
43194CB00006B/535